Be Still

Lori Vaterlaus

Table of Contents

Introduction

I am not an author by trade. I am someone who has been through a very difficult experience and learned a few things at the hand of God. The idea to write a book has been continually swirling around my head for some time now and it will not subside, so I am beginning. Maybe I am to write this for my own benefit. Maybe it will benefit a child of mine, or a grandchild. I only know that there is a story inside me that must come out. It won't be an easy one to tell, at least at first, because it is painful and it is very real. I have learned some difficult lessons, and maybe some of those lessons will in some way help another who is in pain. I do not have all the answers. Even after my experience, maybe *especially* after my experience, I am not in any way an expert in how to endure or how to find peace. I only know my story, my experience, and how my peace came. I hope it helps you. One thing I do know for sure is that when we experience pain we gain compassion, and because of this I have great compassion for you, the reader. I love you without even knowing you and I want your heart to find the peace it needs to heal. May the Lord guide my fingers as I type this to say something that will speak to your heart. As someone who is always setting goals and always has a purpose for everything she does, it's odd to start a project without knowing why. But then again, it's been an odd year.

In order for you to understand how I came to "Be Still" and really know in my heart that God was there, you'll need to understand how my life unraveled. You'll need to understand my story. I'll share a portion of what our family went through in 2009 as we faced one major difficulty after another. I think it wasn't each difficulty that devastated us, it was the fact that all of the difficulties arose within a 12 month period, leaving no time to adjust to the new terror before another was at our feet. I remember well waking each morning wondering which pain would need dealing with, wondering which pain would grab my heart and throw me back into hysteria and leave me completely unproductive in dealing with anything at all. Questions were coming to my mind quicker than I could answer them. They were questions I had never had before, but they were questions that mattered, really mattered. How can I feel God's love when I feel nothing but pain? How do I go forward when I can't seem to get direction as to where to go or what to do? Where do I find strength to continue? What do I do when life gets too hard and I fail? When does it all work out? What about the life I had envisioned for myself? Would it ever come to be? I had the questions, just none of the answers.

Through the grace of God, I managed to find the answers to all of these questions. I found light and truth as I had never known it before. I found that there were tangible, real things I could do that would empower me to know with a surety that the answers I received were directly for me and my situation, and that I *did* know what to do and where to go next. The answers sometimes surprised me. They always challenged me. I found a new way of looking at life. A new way of trusting life. A new way of accepting and loving myself.

1

When Everything Changed

Our family was like most families, I suppose. My husband and I married young. I was 18 and he was 22. We were hopelessly in love and believed that love could conquer just about anything. We had two daughters whom we loved fiercely and did our best to raise them to be productive human beings with good self esteem. I did all I could to stay home with them when they were young. I cleaned houses, provided day care and studied to become a nurse. When they were in school, I went to nursing school and became a nurse. My husband was a hard worker and did a wonderful job balancing his responsibilities at work, home and church. We struggled at times financially, but we were able to own a home and meet the girl's needs.

Throughout the years, we struggled, living paycheck to paycheck, had occasional health problems, and experienced heartache in regards to a child who lived a dangerous lifestyle. Our hearts had known both love and pain. I suppose we really weren't that different from other people. We were just trying to raise a family, be good Christians and offer something to the world.

My husband and I had both come from strong and loving families. They were not without their own problems, but for the most part they were functional and we considered ourselves blessed to have the support of caring families and friends. We knew of many others who had it far worse than we did and so we felt blessed. Each day we would get ourselves up and face the day with hope and courage. Each day we would pray for life's difficulties to resolve and for blessings we knew we needed. Each day we were busy working, volunteering, studying, and trying to raise happy children. In our busyness, we thought we were doing all we could do. We thought life was teaching us all we needed to know, but the tutoring was about to go into hyper speed. Life was going to change, and quickly.

Summer in St. George, Utah is full of clear blue skies, red rock mountains and heat that radiates off those beautiful red rock mountains all day and all night. The summer of 2008 was no different. I was overwhelmed one morning with discouragement and fear concerning one of my daughters. For nearly a decade, I had watched this beloved child of mine struggle with depression and anxiety. We had tried everything, including doctors, therapists, and medication, but she continued to make poor choices and was now living back home with us and her young daughter, our first grandchild.

It was in this desperate state of mind that I went to our temple and prayed that the Lord would give me some insight into the worry I felt for her. A few hours later, at home that day, she told me that she had been raped. Not once, but three times over the years she had been attacked. The shock and horror I felt as she told me of her traumatic experiences nauseated me. As a parent, I was filled with terrible new emotions, but under it all, I knew my prayer had been answered. This was the insight into her behavior. This was the missing piece of the puzzle.

Our family struggled to deal with this when a few months later I got the call from my Mom. She called to tell me that she had found a lump in her groin area. She was sure it was nothing, but at the doctor's insistence she was having it removed. After removing it, the doctors began a series of testing that continued for months and caused much anxiety for Mom and all of those that loved her. With each test, we got closer to the terrible knowledge that our 64-year-old energetic, beautiful mom was dying of cancer.

They would never find the site of origin, but by the time she found that lump, the cancer had spread to her lymphatic system, her liver and her lung. I will never forget hearing the words of the pathology report. Each word pierced my heart and soul with such intense pain. As a nurse, I knew it was grim. As a Christian, I knew a miracle was possible. For months I passed back and forth between those two realities. My Mom was dying and God could perform a miracle. I was on an emotional roller coaster and it exhausted me, but I tried to stay positive for mom and support her the best way I knew how. I put my life on hold and traveled to Springville, Utah to move in with my parents in January 2009.

Mom began chemotherapy in Salt Lake City and I drove her there and sat beside her as she faced the frightening treatment. What a brave lady she was. Trying to keep her sense of humor and share her beautiful smile with everyone, she taught me what true courage was. The chemo immediately took its toll. She was weaker than I had ever seen her, and she slept most of each day. Although she had not appeared sick in any way at the time of diagnosis, she looked sick and old once treatment began. It scared me to see what the drugs did to her - not just the hair loss and nausea, but the weight loss and severe fatigue. The chemo was supposed to get her extra time to enjoy her life but it only robbed her of her quality of life. Once chemo began, in some ways I had already lost my Mama.

On her "good" days, we would try to get a few things done and help her adjust to the knowledge that she was dying and would be leaving her family in 6 to 12 months. There was much she wanted to get done, but between the fatigue and the occasional denial, we weren't very productive. One thing that made her smile was the idea of going with her husband and children on a cruise.

Mom and Dad always worked, I mean *always*. They were either working at their jobs, or working on their home and yard. I think Mom regretted this a little and the thought of taking a fabulous vacation with her family was exciting. We also planned a "Celebration of Life" family reunion to be held in St. George for Easter, Mom's favorite holiday.

Along with planning, we cleaned out linen closets and went through boxes and boxes of old photographs. I didn't know at the time, but these days with Mom would turn out to be one of the greatest blessings of my life. I had intended on staying at Mom and Dad's house most of the year, enjoying what time we had left with each other, planning to make some dreams come true for Mom and helping her with the big projects of going through a lifetime of "things" and giving away and organizing. Sometime around the last week of January things changed dramatically.

My daughter, who was now dealing with post-rape therapy, attempted suicide. She was unsuccessful and the event scared her enough to be serious about a medication change and increased therapy. I felt so torn between needing to be with my mom and needing to be with my daughter. These were very different but equally dramatic needs of people who I loved very much. My husband assured me that he would be there for our daughter and I could stay with my mom. I was surprised when he suddenly showed up at my Mom's house and told me I was no longer staying there. I feared the worst, thinking our daughter was dead. I got hysterical and demanded he tell me what was going on. I didn't think life could get much worse, but it was about to.

After we got in the car, he reassured me that our daughter was OK, but that he had some very disturbing news. He told me that my 10-year-old niece had come forward and said that for the last three years she had been sexually molested by her Grandpa - my dad. Within minutes of my husband telling me this, we were meeting with my sister in a hotel room for one of the worst conversations we would ever have. She filled me in on the despicable details of the living hell her daughter had endured since she was only 7 years old.

My head was spinning. My sweet niece. How I loved her and how my heart ached for her. My beloved mother. Was her 6-month life expectancy not enough heartache? Now she would hear that her husband of 47 years had been sexually molesting their own granddaughter. My own father. Was he the father I had always known, or was he an evil monster? Were my own daughters victims as well?

The questions flooded my thoughts and my stomach revolted. We spent hours with my sister and then assured her that we would do whatever it took to help both her and her daughter. We hugged and cried. Our life as we knew it was unraveling fast.

The four hour drive home to St. George was a blur. I cried mostly. I stared out the window in shock. I didn't want to leave my Mama. I needed to get home quickly for my daughter to be safe. How would I navigate these waters? I had no idea. My husband held my hand and we let it all sink in.

Because of the extreme danger of leaving our daughter alone, I was needed at home more than ever. My sisters dealt with telling Mom and getting my niece both legal and professional help. For the next few months, my days were consumed with conversations on the phone. Trying to handle things in St. George while also supporting my siblings and my mom seemed to take up every minute of each day. First my father denied it, then he said he had made a small mistake, then he admitted to it all. My mom was devastated and confused, and the chemo continued.

All the experiences in my life so far hadn't prepared me for facing Mom's cancer, my daughter's rape and attempted suicide, and my father's pedophilia. Or had they? I knew there was only one I could turn to. My Savior. I began to know in a very personal way what the scriptures talk of when they speak of the rock we must build our foundation on. Surely the storms of life and hell were beating upon me now. Was my foundation built on sand or stone? At this point, I wasn't sure I knew. I prayed as I had never prayed, read the bible daily finding strength in its verses, and found a special closeness to Jesus. He had been there for me at other times in my life, and I knew he would be there for me now.

February through July were awful. Because Mom had chosen to stay with Dad, and Dad could no longer be around the children in the family, the "Celebration of life" family reunion and the family cruise were cancelled. Years of difficult emotions resurfaced and I was having a hard time. Dad remained at the house, so now I couldn't be with my Mama as she was dying. I'm the nurse in the family. It was supposed to be my responsibility and honor to care for my Mom. She was confused and just wanted us all to forgive and forget and be together as a family. It broke her heart that we would not accept Dad and love and help him through this difficult time. The tension was intense and the entire family was hurting.

My siblings and I spoke often about how to deal with all of our feelings without alienating each other. We had lost enough, and losing our close relationships was something we did not want. It would be difficult, but we decided to allow each other to grieve and deal with anger in our own ways and to be patient with each other. As of this writing, we have all done this. We don't all feel the same way on the same day, but we have allowed each other the right to get through the experiences of life our own way. I love my brother and sisters so very much. I hope we always feel this love toward each other.

Because of the chemo, the stress, and the cancer, Mom never did regain her strength and quality of life. Her last months were full of pain. I think the physical pain of cancer did not even compare to the intense emotional pain she endured. Instead of enjoying her family during the last months of life, she saw her children and

husband become estranged from each other. Her beloved husband was now going to be alone after she died.
This caused her great concern. I love my mother with all
my heart. I would have given anything to make her com-
fortable during this time, but I was unable and unwilling
to act as if nothing had happened to my niece. I felt in
my heart that my niece deserved to have others show their
understanding of what had happened to her. I suppose
this was because I never felt anyone ever showed me that
they believed me when I told about my history of abuse
from my father. It's complicated and very hard to put in
to words, but I found myself not wanting to ever see or
speak to my father again.

Mom returned to her Heavenly Father on her birth-
day, July 13th. Days before her death, we were able to say
good-bye to her and sit at her bedside as her children and
husband. It wasn't anything at all like she would have
wanted it, or we would have wanted it. We tried to come
to her bedside with only love in our hearts, setting aside
the upcoming legal actions. When it was my turn to say
good-bye, tears overtook my words. They spilled onto
Mom's beautiful face and she smiled at me and stroked
my face with her hand.

"Mama, I don't think there are any words you and I
haven't already said". She nodded and I felt full love and
closeness between us.

I realized that my entire life I had enjoyed either being with her, calling her on the phone or emailing her
daily. I was so grateful that we had a relationship that had

always been full and open. I had never held back my feelings of love and I had always received love from her. "I'm going to miss you so much" I choked. Then I laid beside her in bed with my head on her chest and cried like the child of hers I was. That time alone with my mother was both painful and beautiful. I cried in her arms and felt the kind of pain that escapes words. It took every ounce of strength in me to get up, kiss her beautiful face and walk out her door. We both knew it would be our last moment on this earth together.

July 13th early in the morning the phone rang. Caller ID showed me it was my dad. That could only mean one thing.

"Hello," I said.

"She's gone," was all he said.

"Thank you for calling me," I replied. I hung up. I now had lost both of my parents. Dad went to jail a month after we buried Mom.

I had two months to cry before the next surprise came. One day while I was at Michael's craft store looking for a frame to surround my favorite picture of my Mom, my husband called my cell phone. He sounded cheerful enough wanting to meet me for a chat, but it was two in the afternoon and he was at work. I thought that was odd. We sat together in the sun on a bench outside of Michael's.

"Today at work, they told me they were downsizing me." I'm not sure I really understood what my husband was saying about his 11 year career with this company.

The sun felt hot and my eyes started to sting. I suppose I had just about had enough because I broke down in tears right there in public. I stared at the ground while Michael tried to comfort me, but all I remember him saying was "I can handle anything Lori except you crying." His love for me was so strong that feeling he had disappointed me in some way was more than he could bear. I took a deep breath, dried my eyes and realized I needed to go to work full time. The time of grieving for my parents needed to be postponed.

The country was suffering from the worst recession in history and many of our friends had been laid off. After two pay cuts in the last year, and after having survived several lay offs, we should have known this was a possibility. So, why were we so surprised? I think because in the back of our minds we really didn't think the Lord would allow us to be faced with yet another challenge.

My husband and I both know that jobs, money, and possessions are not what's important in life, but if we hadn't known that before, the events of the last year had surely taught us that. But, the nine months of unemployment we were about to live through were some of the hardest on us. We so desperately needed to grieve and focus our attention on healing our family, yet each day was full of financial decisions, endless hours at the computer applying for jobs, and networking. Being out of work wasn't as devastating as loosing loved ones by any means, but it was urgent and a constant worry. Watching the money disappear from savings, the food storage shelves become empty, and not knowing how long it would be before he found another job, seemed to be all it took to tip us over the edge. Just when I needed to tend to my own needs, I found myself needing to work full time.

Any of these life challenges would have been difficult on their own, but to face rape, suicide, cancer, death, incest, abuse, prison, and unemployment all within one year was an amazing load to bear. Very quickly I learned that I only had two choices. I could become bitter, or I could become better.

I chose to become better. I have to be honest, it is a daily choice and I am still struggling on that road to recovery. Like I mentioned before, I don't have all the answers. But, I am learning a few things along the way about life, about myself, and mostly about the grace of God. It is for this purpose that I am writing this book. I guess I'm hoping to help someone else along their thorny path. So, here are a few questions I found myself asking, and some of the answers I have come to.

2

How Do I feel God's Love When I feel Nothing But Pain?

ll my life, I had been taught that God would always be near me, no matter what, and, that if I didn't feel His presence in my life then I had moved away from Him, not Him away from me. When I couldn't feel His love and tenderness around me in the midst of all that was going on, I felt I must be doing something wrong. Maybe I was doing too much of one thing, or not enough of another thing. I started doing more of the things I thought I was supposed to be doing and less of the things I thought I wasn't supposed to be doing, but I was only becoming more discouraged and exhausted.

I knew there were others who were looking to me to know how to handle life's challenges. It was important to me that my daughters see an appropriate way to deal with stress. (Isn't it amazing that we as mothers always need to be teaching?) I really did want to show my faith in the way I was dealing with these challenges. I wanted others to know that there was hope when all else showed otherwise, but I wasn't feeling hope. On a bad day, I felt insecure, frightened, angry, sad, confused and hopeless. On a good day, I felt numb. Clearly, what I was doing wasn't working, and I needed something to work soon.

When we feel spiritual things, we know that they are true. We know it because we feel it. That's easy enough. I know God loves me because I can feel it in my heart. I know He hears my prayers because I feel an answer to my prayer. I know my sins are forgiven because I feel the weight of those sins disappear. I know God's will because he speaks to my heart and I feel what I need to do. We get used to being directed by the spirit because we feel the spirit near us so often. What are we to do when those feelings are gone?

I began to think about when Christ asked the Father "My God, my God, why have you forsaken me?" (Matthew 27:45) Had the Father really left him? Had the Father really turned his back on his suffering son? As I asked myself these questions, I learned that faith is acting upon beliefs we have, even when our feelings are confusing us. Maybe for some this is not a new concept, but for me it was.

I realized that real faith isn't always directed by our current feelings. It's more than feelings. Faith is a knowledge that we rely on when life brings out the most overwhelming emotions. It's easy to have faith when you have constant proof, but faith takes on a different meaning when it is something you actively choose. I started choosing to believe that God had not left my side, even though I could no longer feel Him. I started choosing to believe that the Lord Jesus was the only one who could save my family and that He was perfectly capable of making all things right.

I started choosing to trust that Jesus would take all things I felt were causing me harm and use them for my benefit. Not because I could feel these things in my heart, but because I knew that they were true. If they had been true before, they were true now.

As a nurse, I was aware of a phenomenon called the closed gate theory. This is when pain receptors are blocked by other sensory receptors. When a woman is in the pain of childbirth, a gentle caressing of her abdomen will decrease her pain sensation. The theory here is that there are only so many pain receptors and if some of them can be blocked by the tactile caressing, then there is less of a sensation of pain. Could this physical theory be true in a spiritual sense as well? If our spiritual pain receptors are so full at some point, could it be possible that we just aren't capable of feeling, or receiving, anything else? Even good things?

I had faith that my loving Father in Heaven loved me and wanted to help me in my time of need, so was it possible that He was still there beside me even though I was in enough pain to block out any other feelings? Instead of torturing myself with feelings of inadequacy - (was I not doing enough of this, or too much of that?) - I chose to have faith that God really was still there beside me. I chose to believe that His infinite love for me was eternal and that it was not based on how much or how little I did of any one particular thing. In a way, I chose to let myself off the hook. To be gentle with myself. To love myself. To comfort myself.

Certain scriptures took on a precious new meaning for me. I poured over them like lifesaving medicine that would cure my dying heart and spirit. "Come unto me, all ye that labor and are heavy laden, and I will give you rest. Take my yoke upon you, and learn of me: for I am meek and lowly in heart: and ye shall find rest unto your souls. For my yoke is easy and my burden is light." (Matthew 11:28-30)

" But even the very hairs of your head are all numbered. Fear not therefore: Ye are of great value" (Matthew 10:30) "I will not leave you comfortless, I will come to you" (John 14:18) "These things I have spoken unto you, that in me ye might have peace. In the world ye shall have tribulation: but be of good cheer; I have overcome the world." (John 16:33)

If you are like most people I know, then I am going to tell you that you are already doing enough. Your loving, perfect Savior accepts you and your life and is closer to you than you may think. You just may have circuit overload when it comes to your pain receptors! Let yourself off the hook! Stop trying to find a reason that you are no longer feeling those warm fuzzies of the spirit. Let your faith take over. Think back to a time when you were feeling those warm fuzzies and know that it is all still true. You may just be in the eye of the storm where the pain is so intense that you aren't going to feel warm and fuzzy about anything right now. The good news is, the storm will pass, or at least let up for a spell, and those pain receptors will become vacant again and you will feel the intense love of your Father in Heaven once more. Remember, this is what faith is: Believing in something true that you can not see or feel.

Sometimes when we read a scripture over and over, we begin to feel we know it so well that we stop actually focusing on it's meaning. We start to read it, and then our minds say, "yeah, yeah, yeah...I know that one well enough to finish it off by memory."

The miraculous nature of scripture is that it has different meanings for different times in our lives. That's why scriptures can heal us. It's almost as if they have a hidden meaning that we discover at just the right moment. They just comfort us at exactly the time we need them to. God's word is available to bring us a message that we need to hear at exactly the right time we need it.

When you are unable to feel God's love in your heart, and you are worried about yourself or your family, read this message as if for the first time, "For God so loved the world, that he gave his only begotten son, that whosoever believeth in him should not perish, but have everlasting life. For God sent not his son into the world to condemn the world but that the world through him might be saved." (John 3:16-17) That is a message to you. The God of the universe loves you, and he does not want you to feel condemned. His son came to save you and your family, not condemn you and your family. He is your loving Father in Heaven. Feel this truth if you can, and if you can't feel it, *know it*!

The storm of life is nearly unbearable at times, but there is one who loves you in an unfailing, perfect way. He never intended you to go through the pain alone. He planned that you would turn to Him and know He was there for you. "Be strong, do not fear; your God will come, he will come with vengeance; with divine retribution he will come to save you." (Isaiah 35:4)

At the time of this writing, my storm has not passed. Some days it has let up some, and some days I am back in the eye of the storm. On the days that the sunshine of my life is out, I feel His warmth and love flooding over me. I feel Him gently asking me to be patient in my suffering. I feel Him promising me that He will do His job perfectly. He will save my family, heal our hearts, turn these evils into something that will benefit us all. Some days, I just need to remember those feelings and choose to have faith because I, too, am on circuit overload.

3

How Do I Go Forward When I Can't Seem to Get Direction?

As believers in Christ, we learn early on that He is alive and willing to guide our lives if we but ask.

"Ask and it shall be given you, seek and ye shall find; knock and it shall be opened unto you. For everyone that asketh receiveth; and he that seeketh findeth; and to him that knocketh it shall be opened." (Luke 11:10)

I believed this with all my heart. If I ever needed personal revelation and inspiration from heaven, it was now. I needed to make decisions about how to care for my daughter. I needed to make decisions concerning my father and his participation in my family. I needed to know

how I should act, what I should say, and what I should do.
I don't think I had ever been so confused and frightened
in my life. I had lost both parents within six months. I
had nearly lost my daughter and was still living with the
fear that I would lose her at any time. We needed to make
a decision to stay in Utah and hope my husband would
find a job, or move and hope he would find something in
another state. To make matters worse, my physical health
was taking the brunt of the emotional stress and it had
been months since I had slept longer than a few minutes
at a time, and just as long since I was able to tolerate food.
My body's exhaustion and ill health was making it hard to
concentrate and make any decisions all. Even small, every
day decisions seemed blurry state. I needed help. Divine
help. I needed answers and I needed them immediately. I
was willing to go forward and do as the Lord wanted, but I
just couldn't seem to hear Him. How was I to go forward
if I couldn't tell which direction forward was?

My usual method of handling stress is to find a way
to serve others and stay the course.. My husband and I
were currently serving in our church in time-consum-
ing, fulfilling positions that were dear to our heart. We
had lived in our neighborhood for 15 years and loved the
people we served in that area. Much to our disappointment, the neighbors seemed less than interested in our
struggles and our clergy became critical of how we were
handling things with our daughter. These disappointments came at a time when we felt we really needed the
support of others. It devastated us. A few good friends

stood by us, but the people we had served with for those 15 years never made any attempts to come by our home or pray with us -something we desperately needed.

Because I had lost both parents, the support of my church friends, my neighbors and my clergy, I found myself without anyone to turn to. My brother and sisters were struggling to keep their lives and families together as I was. They loved me dearly, I knew that, but they did not live near by and they were struggling too. My husband was working harder than ever before trying to find a job now that unemployment was running out, so he was preoccupied. I found myself completely and utterly alone. It forced me towards my Savior as not only my God, but my friend and confidant. I made the difficult decision to resign from my service in the church for a time, and to focus on dealing with the legal issues facing my family and the hard work of healing a broken heart. Looking back on it now, I am sure that I would not have relied so heavily on my Savior for support if there had been others there to support me. It was He and I!

I talked to Him throughout the day, every day. Each morning as I was laying in bed for hours before the sun came up, I spoke with Him in the most intimate way. He was my everything. Parent, friend, spouse, clergy, and the only one I could rely on. I found out quickly that I could trust Him with all of my thoughts. He was listening, not judging me. He was allowing me to use him as my sounding board and counselor both. He was a great therapist!

With my husband's unemployment came huge changes in our activities of daily living. The T.V. service was now gone, as was the occasional date night, shopping, and social life. Without these noises of life, and without the busy schedule I was used to, life became very quiet. For the first time, life became extremely quiet. Quiet enough, in fact, that I began to listen for things I hadn't heard before.

Take a minute right now and ask yourself this question: How quiet is my life? If your answer is something like, "yeah, right" or, "you've got to be kidding me" I relate. I loved my life of noise and service and family and friends and career and marriage and travel and humanitarian service and study and fun! It was a great life, but it was definitely not quiet. Once my life became quiet, I could hear. But how do you quiet a productive and busy life? How is that possible? Well, for me, it was taken from me. I lost everything that was causing the noise and I was left with nothing. One of the first things I heard in my quest for direction was the message to be patient. In the midst of my unbearable pain and anguish, this is not what I wanted to hear, but, it was clear as could be. "Be patient and know that I am working a great work here." The next message I heard was, "Be still, and know that I am God" (Psalm 46:10) *Be still*.

I could not really know that God was in charge until I was, first, very still. My life had to nearly stop before it was quiet enough for me to learn that God is not surprised by all that is happening in our lives. He is not shocked with horror as we are. He is not panicked like we are when things seem to be falling apart all around us. He is in charge! He has it covered. He is prepared. He knows what to do and what not to do. But we will never feel his omnipotent power of control in our lives unless we are still.

It was Jesus who said, "If thou canst believe, all things are possible to him that believeth." (Mark 9:23) And, "With men it is impossible, but not with God: For with God all things are possible." (Mark 10:27) Then there is His promise of "Peace I leave with you, my peace I give unto you; not as the world giveth, give I unto you. Let not your heart be troubled, neither let it be afraid." (John 14:27) These are not the words of someone who is panicking over what is going on in our homes or in the world. Our Lord has complete control over every situation and he will use all things for our good if we trust in Him. In order for us to be consoled by his words and taught by him, we must be still.

There are two parts to being still. The first one is obvious. We must learn to turn the noise down, or find a place to just be where it is quiet. This must happen on a regular basis and occur long enough for the second part: The stillness on the inside. As hard as it is to control the noise on the outside of our lives, it is even more difficult to quiet ourselves on the inside. Have you ever been up in the middle of the night when all is quiet in the house, but your head is so noisy you can't think or sleep? Just finding a quiet place is not enough for the spirit to speak to us and comfort us. We must find a way to quiet our insides as well. Although there is not one recipe only for inner quiet, I have found three steps that will work for just about anyone.

Step One - Eliminate Negativity

> Start by eliminating anything that is dark in nature and causes you to feel stressed or emotionally upset in any way. Because we cannot just quit our families, or jobs, or life, eliminate the "extras". At first, I felt there was nothing in my life that I could eliminate. After my husband's income stopped, we let go of everything extra and some of that was negative and dark. Without knowing it, movies and music that were emotionally charged in nature were causing us more upset. Reality shows, intense films, emotional music about difficulties in life, and especially the daily news were all contributing to our inner noise. Now, I'm not suggesting that any of us give up these things permanently, but I am suggesting that in times of deep stress, and when we need to feel the spirit actively helping us know how to move forward, it can be very helpful to do without some of these things.

Step Two - Choose Positivity

With these negative things gone, there is room now for more positivity. For me, at least, just removing the negative things left me with the voice in my head that was worrying and wondering what to do. I needed to quiet that voice in my head with something positive. I turned to beautiful Christian music with lyrics that spoke of Christ's love for me. I needed gentleness and these songs comforted me throughout each day. I remember hearing one of my daughters talk of "Mom's Jesus songs" as if I was going a little over the top by only listening to that one CD of a collection of my favorite songs of grace. I'm a huge music lover of all kinds of music. So, usually I listen to quite an eclectic collection. But during this time of my life, it was just that one CD. I had all of the words memorized and I listened and sang and worshipped to that one CD for over a year. Sound a little obsessive? Well, maybe it was. But, the words of those songs brought me to a very basic level of understanding. I began to understand just how very simple it is to accept my Savior and have him in my life as my constant and dearest friend. All the complications that we as people bring to religion and philosophy began to fade away and I was left with the simple truth that my Savior loved me. During times of great stress in life, I think it's easy for us to complicate further our already complex issues. These simple songs of praise kept my mind from complicating my situation further and worrying over things that I had no control over. For at least a year I drove around running my errands, singing these simple songs, and allowing them to not only heal my breaking heart but quiet my insides.

I did the same thing with the books that I read. I love a great biography or an exciting novel, but those remained on the shelf with the eclectic music library. I only read books that spoke love and goodness to my heart. Hundreds of authors have written books of hope, and since nights seemed to be the hardest for me, I kept a book beside my bed and read it each night until I fell asleep. If I awoke in the night, I picked the book back up and read some more. Sometimes these books were scripture itself, other times they were from Christian authors, but they always contained messages that were positive and encouraging. This too quieted my insides. The voice of worry and panic in my head was calming, and I was allowed to hear that quiet voice of God I so desperately was seeking.

Along with replacing music and books, I incorporated positive activities into each day. Sometimes it was quiet service of others that brought me peace. Sometimes it was a walk in nature to feel the grandeur of God's work. Since life and it's responsibilities doesn't ever stop, I needed to make time for these positive activities. Sometimes, that meant saying no to good things and allowing time for better things. It wasn't like me to take time to myself and go meditate in nature. I always felt that it was a great idea, but I was just too busy for something like that, and I just couldn't justify it. But, in my intense grief, I made the time and the healing and clarity of mind started to come.

One particularly difficult day, I drove myself to Zion National Park and checked into a hotel alone. This was a first for me. Moms just don't pack up and take themselves on a trip alone. I cried the whole way there feeling guilty that my husband was looking so worried when I pulled out of the driveway. I felt guilty that my daughter and my granddaughter might need something while I was away and I wouldn't be there for them. And mostly, I felt guilty that I was spending money that we didn't really have on a hotel room. After I cried for hours in the hotel room feeling like a miserable wife and mother, I was quiet inside and God spoke to my heart in two amazing ways.

I got up from the bed and walked to the window. The hotels at Zion have these amazingly huge glass windows so you can look out onto the beautiful rock mountains that the park is so well known for. With swollen eyes I gazed up at an enormous and stunning sandstone landscape that took my breath away.

"If I can create all of this Lori, I can handle your problems" were the words God laid on my heart at that moment. I had left the noise and he was right there to speak to me. I knew I must turn things over to him. The problems were out of my control and I wasn't making things any better by trying to hang on to them and fix them myself. He was in control, as He always had been, and He was asking me gently to trust Him with it all.

The next lesson came the following morning. I walked until I didn't feel like walking anymore and then I sat down at the edge of the Virgin river. I think I sat there most of the morning just being still. Staring at the currents of water rushing by, I thought of nothing. Not how to help someone, or how to fix something, or what I could be doing better, or why things had turned out the way they did. I was thinking of absolutely nothing when I saw a twig come floating down the river just in front of me. I watched as it floated along slowly until it got caught up in some little rapids and finally a whirlpool where it stayed for quite awhile, spinning around and around and getting sucked under and tossed about. I thought to myself how my life had been a lot like this twig. I was on course too, but had been caught up in a terrible whirlpool that kept drowning me and preventing me from getting back on course. Just as I thought this, the twig suddenly escaped the whirlpool, shot out of the water and landed back in the river a good foot or two downstream. I smiled to myself. Then, another twig caught my eye a few feet up river. I watched this one as well, as it was along the same route floating down the river, but it managed to avoid the whirlpool. Its current carried it a different way and it slowly moved around a rock or two and continued on it's gentle course. It never got caught up in the turbulent whirlpool, but it also never shot out with great force, gaining a foot or two. It was slower. Never changing. Never challenged. Never jetting forth from the water with great strength.

"This whirlpool in your life, Lori, will propel you farther and faster in my work for you than if you had kept cruising along without these challenges," He spoke again.

Since those few days in nature, I have heard him speak over and over to my heart. He has guided me through some terrible times and helped me each day to know his will. I suppose he was always there, but with the noise turned up so loud on the inside and on the outside, I just couldn't hear him.

Step Three - Be Patient in Listening

After I got quiet and felt the stillness, God continued to speak to me and the fog that had clouded over my life began to lift. I began to move forward, doing the things I needed to do slowly each day. The answers didn't come immediately for me, but I began to feel comfort in knowing that I could make the decisions I needed to make with a new confidence that God was at my side and in charge. I'd always heard about God's timing, but I began to understand this concept in a very new way. Because God's timing is eternal, it's really OK to move slowly at times. In times of intense pain, I would really prefer to get it over with quickly but I learned that God may just need me to endure the experience. As I continued listening to Him, I had the thought, "be patient."

In my spiritual journey throughout life, I had always focused on my personal relationship with my Savior and my personal purpose in life. Then I realized that sometimes I need to understand that it's not always about *me*! In order for God's purposes to happen completely, others need to be involved. I look at it this way: Even though a particular experience may be affecting me profoundly and personally, it may actually be about someone else. Maybe my job is simply to stay strong even in the midst of the pain. I also learned that not everything is my fault. Not everything can, or should, happen because of my actions. It took me writing this to realize that I really *am* a control freak. Perhaps everyone is to some extent. Deep down we really must understand that our actions have consequences, and they do, but sometimes our actions will simply not give us the consequences we hope and pray for. Sometimes it's just not about us.

When I started listening to this lesson from the Lord, I looked around at others in my life and felt a deep compassion for them. My children, my grandchildren, my sisters and brother, my parents and grandparents all needed to experience and grow just like I did, and I began to hear my Heavenly Father asking me to allow His work to take place and stop resisting it. Trust became critical. "Trust in the Lord with all your heart and lean not unto your own understanding. In all your ways acknowledge Him and He shall direct your paths." (Proverbs 3:5) I'd add to that, "in His own time and ways that are beneficial to all His children, not just you."

Eternity is a very long time, and it just may take a very long time for some things to heal and get better. Sometimes the answer to the question "where do I go God, and what do I do?" is just to be patient and allow God to work his plan for all His children.

4

Where Do I Find the Srength to Continue?

Many of us who are brought up with religious backgrounds are taught at a young age that our strength comes from the Lord. But in our society we are also taught other sources of strength. Do any of these sound familiar?

"The only person you can depend on is yourself!"
"Families are forever and always there for us in times of need."
"A real friend is someone who stands beside you in good times and in bad."

"The vow of marriage is for better and for worse, in sickness and in health."

"You have the power to attract only good and positive into your life."

Although there is some truth to all of these, I think there is also some risk in believing that anything or anyone other than the Lord Jesus Christ will *always* be our source of strength. Our parents, our friends, our children and even our own self will at one time or another let us down. We know that, but we want to believe otherwise, so we do.

Years ago, I was chatting with my mother-in-law on the phone during a time when my husband was undergoing some serious medical testing. I cried to her in my worries and told her that I could survive anything except losing my husband. I was surprised that she responded with a quick, "Oh, you could do it. The only thing you really need is your Savior." I wondered how she could speak of her own son that way. In my 20-something-year-old mind, I told myself that my love for my husband must be greater than anything she had ever experienced. (This is embarrassing to admit now, since my mother-in-law is a woman of great love and depth.) I had no idea what she was really saying. I hadn't yet experienced the pains of life and the disappointments that would lead me to knowing that what she said was true. I only really needed my Savior, and He would be the only one to never disappoint.

If He is the source of our strength, how do we connect to this source? Since we are all unique children of the most high God, I believe we all have unique spirits. So we all must also have unique struggles and abilities, just like our own children who have different ways of learning and growing. No parent would consider parenting every one of their children the same and expect the same results. On the contrary, the challenge of parenting is in knowing how best to meet the needs of each child and teach them in a way they can learn. Our Father in Heaven must know this, too, with His children. To say there is only a handful of ways to tap into the source of our Savior would be shortsighted at best. The planet is full of God's children who all have different needs and different responses to life and learning.

There are things all of God's children can do that can help us see God's love for us and give us strength. All of us can pray and read God's word. There is great power in putting words to our feelings and speaking our innermost thoughts and needs.

I know of people who pray in a formal way of speaking, showing the utmost respect for the God they are praying to. I know of people who talk in the most intimate and casual way to their friend and their redeemer Jesus Christ, telling him of each day and each struggle and victory in their lives. I know others who write their prayers in a prayer journal feeling that they can better express themselves in writing. They use these journals to re-read their own conversations with the Lord and it helps them see their own intentions and desires. I have sat with a dying woman as she prayed her rosary prayers, counting each beloved bead feeling strength from her beloved Jesus. All of these people are sincere in their love and devotion to deity and all gain strength from their practice of turning to God to help them have the strength to continue.

I remember one time in my life when I had been praying for an answer to whether or not we should adopt a little girl named Stephanie who had many medical problems. We loved Stephanie and wanted her to be a part of our family, but we knew we could never afford the multiple surgeries she would need and deserve. I had taken this to my Heavenly Father in prayer many times over several months, but did not feel I had received any answer one way or another as to whether or not we should adopt Stephanie.

I was talking to a friend of mine one day and told her that for something so important I would have thought that God would have answered me by now. She, not so gently, told me that He probably was answering me but I just wanted Stephanie so badly that I wasn't listening. I left her home immediately with my feelings hurt and I went directly to my bedroom and literally fell to my knees. There were no words left to pray.

I cried out loud while looking up to my ceiling. I didn't pray with respectful language, nor did I intimately speak to my Heavenly Father. I didn't write down my deepest desires and I didn't pray a beloved prayer I had been taught as a child. I did pray though, like I had never prayed before. Without words of any kind, I prayed a prayer of tears. God knew every one of my thoughts, desires, intentions and struggles. In the midst of those sobs, he heard and answered, "No, my child."

Paul explained it this way to the Romans. "In the same way, the Spirit helps us in our weakness. We do not know what we ought to pray for, but the Spirit himself intercedes for us through wordless groans." (Romans 8:26)

My wordless groans were heard.

Turning our thoughts, our words, and our groans to Him who is the only one who can give us true strength is universally powerful. One of the reasons other people can not fully understand our pain is because they have not experienced it in the same way.

Even those who have had a similar experience can not completely understand our own individual pain because they are not us. Only the Lord and Savior Jesus Christ has experienced our exact pain. His atonement made it possible for Him to experience every experience every human would encounter. We can not begin to understand how this works, but it did happen. He did indeed go into a garden alone and bleed from every pore as He felt each and every feeling we all would have: Abandonment, guilt, self-loathing, disappointment, shock, horror, hate, bitterness, loneliness and so many more feelings. This was God's plan for His children so that in our own struggles we would know there was one we could reach out to for strength, one that would know every emotion we were feeling. He truly does know how to succor His people. He is the only one who knows how to succor His people. That is why he is the only one we can turn to for strength to continue.

The good news of the gospel is this: all it takes is that first word or that first groan or that first look towards Heaven. Even if you can't form the words, He knows. When you wonder where you can go for the strength to continue, all you have to do is turn towards Him who loves you dearly. He will come rushing to you to encircle you in the arms of His love.

The words we sang at my Mom's funeral explain this well.

"Where can I turn for peace? Where is my solace when other sources cease to make me whole? When with a wounded heart, anger, or malice, I draw myself apart, searching my soul?

Where, when my aching grows, where when I languish, where in my need to know, where can I run? Where is the quiet hand to calm my anguish? Who, who can understand? He, only One.

He answers privately, reaches my reaching in my Gethsemane, Savior and Friend.

Gentle the peace he finds for my beseeching. Constant he is and kind, love without end" ("Where Can I Turn For Peace?, Emma Lou Thane, 1924)

When I was younger, I thought the language of scripture was entirely too difficult to understand. As I read the words, I felt a great spirit there, but as far as being practical in helping me, not so much. In 2009, when my life was falling apart, I turned toward the words in the New Testament with a hunger I had never had before. My daughter bought me a bible that had the words of Christ in red lettering, and I read everything in red.

I feasted on the words Christ had spoken when he was here on the earth. I found meaning in all of it like I never had before. Because life was always more difficult at night when I was tired, I read until I fell asleep each night. I wanted those words of Christ to be the last thing I was thinking of when I fell asleep. Maybe this would take away the nightmares I was having about my father. "If ye continue in my word, then are ye my disciples indeed: And ye shall know the truth, and the truth shall make you free" (John 8:32)

I needed this freedom, and reading His word was freeing my mind from endless thought patterns of entrapment and discouragement. The darkness of my situation seemed a little lighter when I read, "I am the light of the world: he that followeth me shall not walk in darkness, but shall have the light of life." (John 12:46)

I still wanted my situation to be different. Actually, I wanted my situation to have never happened, but it was happening and it was all so dark and negative that reading words of light seemed to stand out in contrast like they never had before.

If you, dear reader, are in a very dark place please know there is light offered in the word of God. He has not forgotten you. In fact, it is written, "He shall give His angels charge over you, to keep you: And in their hands they shall bear you up, lest at any time you dash your foot against a stone." (Psalm 91:11-12)

Dashing our foot against a stone is a small thing, and even in that, His angels are watching over us. Imagine the leagues of angels that are accompanying you when your stone is one of life's great stumbling blocks.

There have been thousands of ideas on how to read the word of God daily. I had done at least a hundred of them. I read a chapter a day, early morning, before bed, with the family, alone, King James, NIV, book on tape, verse a day pads with pretty pictures on them.... the list goes on. All of these are good, but the real good that comes from reading the word of God is when you are starved for it! When every philosophy book, parenting book and self help book fail to give you what you need, when your thirst for answers is far worse than the man lost in death valley thirsts for water, when you are needy and your spirit is crying out for comfort every minute of every day, you will find meaning in these words: "And Jesus said unto them, I am the bread of life. He that comes to me will never hunger, and he that believes me shall never thirst." (John 6:35)

Prayer and reading the word of God are only two of the ways your Father in Heaven will give you the strength to continue, but they are a great place to start. Maybe there will be miracles, maybe there will be people that will come into your life at just the right time, maybe you will just be able to endure when it wouldn't really be possible without God's help. Maybe you'll be aware of the strength He is giving you, maybe you won't, but if you are very honest with yourself, you'll know that He is there for you.

About a year before my personal tragedies started piling on, I was asked to work with a lady named Lyn in the women's ministry of our church. I knew who she was, but didn't know her personally. We worked hard serving the Lord by reaching out to the women of our congregation and trying to listen to their needs. After much thought and prayer on the subject, we had what we thought was a good plan to help the women come together in a spirit of Christ and friendship and we made a lot of plans for the coming years we thought we would be together in this ministry.

We were just getting to know each other well enough to work well together and good things were just starting to happen with the women when my struggles began. I couldn't continue to serve in this capacity while living with my parents, so I sadly had to let it go. At the time, I thought how sad it was that we didn't really get to do all the things we were so excited about. I felt disappointed that I had only had a short time to work with Lyn and get to know her. I had believed that God had brought us together to serve these ladies, and I really didn't get enough time to do that. I chalked it up to just another one of the losses I was having to deal with.

During the last month of her life, Mom came to visit me in Southern Utah. She asked me to take her to meet this Lyn I had been talking about. I was happy to introduce these two ladies because they reminded me so much of each other. They were the same age and full of love in their hearts for the Lord and for the women's ministry. I'll never forget seeing Lyn and Mom standing there meeting each other and hearing Mom's words to Lyn, "I just wanted to meet the lady who will be looking out for my Lori."

With great emotion they looked into each other's eyes and I needed to walk away. At this writing, it's been nearly 3 years since my Mom passed on, and Lyn still calls me and takes me to lunch every single week. She is a dear friend to me, yes, but more than that, she was one who God put in my path at just the right time because He knew I would need her. I thought my opportunity to serve in the women's ministry was for the women, but it was for me. A year before I would need Lyn, God brought her into my life and put us in a situation that we would bond quickly in the service of Christ. All my volunteer hours were really for me. That is how loving our Father in Heaven is. He makes sure that we have all we will ever need, at just the right time. He never leaves us lacking for anything but gives us the strength we will need to continue on.

"And we know that in all things God works for the good of those who love him, who have been called according to his purpose." (Romans 8:28)

5

What Do I Do When Life Gets Too Hard and I Fail?

Maybe it's just a woman thing, but it seems to me that we compare ourselves and our families to others all the time. We see them attending church together in their matching dresses and smiles and assume their mornings were full of I love yous and, "OK, Mom, I'll do that," while we remember the harsh words that were spoken in our own homes that Sunday morning. We have failed in our minds.

We see other couples at restaurants who appear so in love and perfect, and we compare that assumed relationship to our struggling one with our spouse. We have, in our minds of course, figured out that the couple laugh all the time and share a completely trouble free existence. They never argue or feel unsatisfied. They never have any serious troubles face them, and they absolutely never loose their temper. Again, in our minds, we have failed.

We see parents whose children have graduated from college with multiple degrees, served missions in far away lands and speak foreign languages, had lots of beautiful and healthy children and served in many capacities in the community and in their church, and once again in our minds we have failed.

If we do see others struggling, they appear to always be handling their struggles with so much grace and faith. We see them testify of God's goodness even in the midst of terrible challenges, and we think to ourselves, "I don't have anything to complain about and look at me, I'm failing at even living what I believe!"

Everywhere we turn we can see our own failure. We're not enough of this, or too much of that. We never quite measure up to what we expect of ourselves. And the truth is, sometimes we're even told by someone we hold in high regard that we're not measuring up. Sure, they don't use those words exactly, but well meaning people tell us that if we would do more of something or less of something else, then we would get better results. In our minds, we have now just had a second opinion to the negative one we already hold of ourself.

For most of us, it doesn't take long before we think we have failed in every single area of our lives. After believing that we are just simply not good enough, we then jump to the conclusion that we have not only let ourself and others down, but we have let God down too. He must feel about us what others feel about us. Even if we still know at some level that he loves us, we feel we have disappointed Him. Of all the levels of failure, this one is the worst. To disappoint God.

Although I have felt failure many times before, there was one time in particular that I was completely overwhelmed with the feeling that I was not only a poor mother, wife, citizen, and christian, but there wasn't anything of importance I had succeeded in. My feelings of failure had turned into an almost tangible darkness that surrounded me. This feeling lasted for months, and seemed to be getting worse with time. The more failure I felt, the more darkness encircled me. It always seemed to be worse at night when I was tired from the day's struggles. In the quiet hours of the night when everyone else was asleep, I would find myself on the couch crying quietly.

One night in my deep despair, I felt the most powerful message. The Lord laid upon my heart these words:

"I know you have done your very best, and it is enough." Now, those ordinary words came to me with such power that even years later as I write them, tears come to my eyes. I learned something that night. The only opinion that ever really matters is God's, and He has told us that if we come unto him with a pure heart and believe and accept Him as our Savior we will be saved.

"Then they cried to the Lord in their trouble, and he saved them from their distress" (Psalm 107:13) Whatever your distress is, cry to the Lord and He will save you from it.

To answer the question "What do I do when life gets too hard and I fail?" Please hear me, dear reader, you have not failed. You only think you have failed. Jesus Christ has already stepped in to make up for your shortcomings and all you need to do is accept this great act of love. With Him, it is enough. If you are already giving it your all, it is enough. Sure, we can look back at our past and know now that we would do things differently, but we did the best we could with the knowledge and experience we had at the time. With a pure heart, that is enough.

The Lord has, in his infinite wisdom and love, already atoned for it all. Sometimes we hear these words, "Well done, thou good and faithful servant: thou hast been faithful over a few things, I will make thee ruler over many things" (Matthew 25:21) and we define the word "faithful" as perfect.

If our Heavenly Father had thought you had the ability to be perfect, he would not have provided a Savior to atone for your imperfections. He already knew, and was OK with the fact that you would not be capable of doing everything perfectly. Because He is all powerful, He could have done anything, but he chose to create you just as you are, imperfections and all, and His plan for your learning and progress is perfect for you. Your experiences have been tailor-made just to help you learn the

things you need to learn here on this earth. God truly
will make all things work for your good.

If you are feeling like life is just too hard and you
have failed, please be gentle with yourself because God
is. He will gently lead you home to Him through a Savior
who loved you enough to die on the cross for you. Be
gentle to yourself and believe.

6

When Does It All Work Out?

When I look back at my husband's unemployment period, I remember that the hardest part was not knowing how long he would be unemployed. Would it be two months, or two years? If someone had told us that he would be laid off for six months, or 12 months, or 24 months, and then he would find employment after that time, we could have handled it so much better. It was the constant uncertainty of not knowing when it would all work out. As it turned out, it was 9 months. The very week his unemployment benefits were ending, my husband got a new job. Coincidence? I think not. In looking at the situation now, we did just fine. God provided just what we needed just when we needed it. There was never anything extra, and we did not have the knowledge of how and when things would work themselves out, but they did.

Life is much the same. If the single woman who is desperately lonely was told that she would be alone for 10 years, but that then she would find the love of her life, she would get busy during that 10 years and find joy knowing that after that time she would have the husband she wanted. But, it's in the not knowing that she remains lonely, wondering if it will be forever.

There is a story in a popular fiction book (*The Shack* by William P. Young) that describes a man's conversation with God about his teenage daughter whom he is very concerned about. He asks God why He is not worried about the girl like he himself is. God's answer is that he already knows that the girl will fail over and over but on attempt 29 she will succeed. So, God says, He doesn't need to worry about attempts 5, 16 or 28 failing, because He knows that she will eventually succeed, and He knows when.

As much as we don't like it, we don't get to know when it all works out. That's for God to know, not us. But, we do get to know that it *does* all work out. We face evil each day of this life, it's all around us. Good versus evil has been a part of this earthly experience since Adam and Eve. It always will be a part of our earthly journey. But, we never need to concern ourselves with the outcome. God has told us that He will be victorious. Good will win! We can know the outcome of this battle before we choose sides. With perfect knowledge we can choose to be on the winning team! How cool is that? I don't know of any game, match, race, business dealing, or anything else for that matter where we get to know the end from the beginning. This is a no-risk decision. We get to join the guaranteed winning team!

Here's another thing I learned. When I got married and started my family I had this idea in my mind of how things would go. I knew there would be trials, but I still had a vision for my family of how I wanted our lives to be. That's not in itself a bad thing, but here's where I went wrong: When things turned quickly and drastically away from that vision I had for my family, I panicked. I felt things were going terribly wrong. I grasped at straws, so to speak, trying to get things back to the way I thought they were supposed to be.

When my mindset was focused on things that were going wrong, I needed to fix them, and quickly. I felt I had made some awful mistake that had brought all of this on myself and my family, and, if I hadn't made the mistake, then somebody else had. Either way, we had let things get off course and they needed to be brought back into harmony with my idea of what our family life would be. This panic caused me to react too quickly to most things and that wasn't helping the matter. It also made me in some way feel that God was panicking too. He must be looking down from Heaven at our family and thinking, "oh wow, that family is really in trouble now!" This seems silly now, but I can tell you that I must have been thinking God was panicking about my family's undoing.

If I had thought God was completely in charge and was really aware of our situation, I don't think I would have been in such a state of panic. I think I would have been feeling some peace. But I wasn't feeling anything close to peace. I was drowning in panic and dread most days. Then, I was reading an uplifting book by one of my favorite Pastors and another one of God's tender messages fell on my heart.

God was not panicked. He was not nervous. He was not surprised at what was happening in our family. In fact, He had known these things were going to happen long before the wheels were even in motion. Because He knew these experiences would come to our family, He equipped us with everything we would need to get through these experiences. Personally, I don't believe God plays with our lives. I don't believe He intentionally causes evil and hurt to come into our lives just to see how we will react, or to test us in any way. I believe He has set up our world and our existence to allow free choice and agency, and that free choice sometimes results in evil and destructive behavior. Some people choose to harm others. They choose to be selfish. They choose evil over good. But because God is all knowing, He is never surprised by these choices. He sees the end from the beginning and has a plan for each of us to not only survive this life, but feel joy in it!

When I continually remind myself in stressful times that my Heavenly Father has seen it coming and has given me all I need to face the struggles of life, I feel peace.

I may not like what's going on, but I don't resist life like I used to. It takes an amazing amount of energy to fight the flow of life and try to intercept evil and turn it into good all the time. That's why it's God's job, not ours. Only He has the energy and power and authority to govern the world. I think most of us would agree that it's not our job, but somehow we try to do it anyway.

A wise person once told me that I should keep my focus on only two time frames: The *now* and *eternity*. Sometimes tomorrow or next week is just too much to handle. I have found this to be true. Even though I am one of those driven, goal-setting, crazy people, the only way I can survive is to focus on the very minute I am in and the eternity my Lord has promised me. So, for the *now* remember, "But God is faithful, who will not suffer you to be tempted above that ye are able; but will with the temptation also make a way to escape, that ye may be able to bear it." (I Corinthians 10:13) And for the *eternity* remember "Eye hath not seen, nor ear heard, neither have entered into the heart of man, the things which God hath prepared for them that love him." (I Corinthians 2:9)

7

What About the Life I Envisioned For Myself?

I'm a huge goal setter. Ever since I was a little girl who wanted to be an olympic gymnast (doesn't every little girl want that?), I have known how to have a dream and go after it. My coaches made it very clear to me what it would take to achieve every trick. Six days a week, I would be at the gym trying it over and over again. Then the magical day would come. I would stick the landing and jump with joy. Then it would be on to the next trick. I learned that if you want something bad enough, you'll get it with enough hard work and determination. I'm so grateful that I learned this at a young age.

Somewhere along the line though, I missed the memo about not having control over things like cancer, evil, the economy, and anyone else who isn't me. I found that I was actually surprised when life took a turn that wasn't in my Plan A. While I still think it's a great idea to have a vision for our lives and work with incredible tenacity to achieve that vision, I have discovered that in almost all cases Plan B turns out even better. Here are just a few examples:

Mother Teresa was on a train when God spoke to her heart and told her that her purpose for life was to serve the poorest of the poor. - Plan B.

Peter the Apostle was busy working his craft as a fisherman one day when Jesus told him that he would make him a fisher of men. - Plan B.

Greg Mortensen, a registered nurse, was taking a hike one day in Pakistan when he got lost, wandered into a village and promised the people he would build schools for the children. - Plan B.

Oprah Winfrey wanted to be a teacher. She landed a job in news and found her life purpose in front of a T.V. camera. - Plan B.

Today while I was out walking, I thought of all the people who have influenced my life and I couldn't think of one of those people who had actually lived their Plan A. I was so thankful for all of them, and so grateful they had been open to Plan B so I could learn from them.

As I walked in the desert, I let my mind focus on as many great people as I could. I focused on people who really cared about the world and about people, people who in my opinion had really made a difference while on this planet, people I admired. Not a single one of them had stuck with Plan A. God had shown them a better plan; A plan for His purpose. Not all of them had willingly accepted this new plan for their lives. Some had found themselves on a different road by mistake while others had been hurled onto a different path by another person's choices. But, all of them had done marvelous work with their lives. All of them had affected me for good and helped me in some way along my own path. Their example and their life's work had in some way made my journey better.

I grew up in an era of parents teaching their children that they could be anything they wanted to be in this world. They empowered their little girls, in particular, to know they could decide what they wanted to be and study hard and achieve it. I can't remember how many times adults would ask me, "What do you want to be when you grow up?" Being a mother of two daughters myself, I said those same words. I wanted my girls to know that they could be anything they decided they wanted to be. I never once asked them, "What do you think God wants you to be?" or, "What do you think God wants you to do with your life?"

There's nothing wrong with actively creating the life we want to have. There's nothing wrong with empowering children to know they have choice, or teaching them how to set long term goals for their lives. I'll be a goal setter until the day I die, and probably long after that; it moves me to action and is the catalyst to accomplishment. If we could go after all the dreams we wanted with the knowledge that along the way there might be something better, imagine the possibilities! For many of us, there's some down-time after Plan A has collapsed before we actually accept Plan B. If we were open to the idea that God might have another plan for us, we could recognize it quicker and not take it so hard when the original dream dissipated.

Joel Osteen once said that while praying, he always asks God for what he wants, or for something better. How many of us aren't interested in the something better? We just want what we want and that's all there is to it. We pray with full heart and soul for the things we want so desperately to arrive in our lives, and then occasionally say, "Thy will be done". But we really don't want His will to be done if it's different than our own. We'll settle for it if we have to and endure it to the end, by golly, but it's not our first choice, that's for sure! What if we actually *did* trust our Heavenly Father enough to know that His will for us would bring us the absolute most joy? What if when we started to see our desires and wishes not coming to be, we actually looked towards the Plan B with an open mind and heart knowing that what was coming was far better than what we had started out for anyway?

If you, beloved reader, are in a situation now where your life looks nothing like the one you envisioned when you were 10, you are in good company. God has some-thing great in store for you and those you love. It may not look anything like what you wished for, prayed for, or dreamed about, but it is glorious! You may be right in the middle of the remodeling of your life and want to shout, "But this is awful and I don't want it!"

Yes, dreams are hard to give up, especially when they involve those we care deeply about. Think of it this way: If the Lord Jesus came to have lunch with you today and told you he would personally see to it that you and every-one you love would have exactly what they needed in this life and He would bring you all home to Him, would you take Him up on it? If He told you it might not look at all like you envisioned it, but that he would be in charge of it, would you trust Him? He has indeed told us these things. He has a plan and a purpose for each one of us, and it is uniquely formed to give us and our loved ones exactly what we need in life and bring us home to Him. His plan just may look a little different (or a lot differ-ent) than the one we had for ourselves.

One of the greatest blessings in my life is my amazing granddaughter. She came to our family under circum-stances I would have never hoped for. At times, my heart cried out to my Heavenly Father in such intense worry and pain that I was sure nothing good was going to come of our situation. Nothing I prayed for happened at that time. My reality was so different than what I had thought it could ever be, and then, there she was! She is the great-est gift God could ever bring our family. He knew exactly what our family needed and He provided her. She came, as all angels do, on God's errand of love. She has transformed our family and brought such love and grace to us all. I am overwhelmed with gratitude to a God who gave me what we needed and not what I asked for. What I was asking for in those prayers wasn't wrong, but I had forgotten the part about "or something better!"

8

The Good News

The word gospel is derived from an old anglo-saxon word meaning "good message" or "good news". I don't know about you, dear reader, but I know that when I'm in the eye of the storm I look for *any* good news. Sometimes the gospel is the only good news there is. Looking to the world, or to my family, or to my friends does not offer the good news I'm looking for. Many times, the only peace, solace or comfort I find is in the good news the Lord has for me. He offers the good news that He has overcome all and made it possible for me to overcome all as well. He offers the good news that His love is eternal and never changing for me. He offers the good news that in a world that is always changing, He is constant. He offers the good news that even when my world is crashing down around me, He is the solid rock I can stand firm on.

As I mentioned earlier, I have not completely healed from the events of 2009. I'm not sure I will ever completely heal from those events, at least not in this life time. I still find myself on some very dark days, struggling to go forward in a healthy way, but most days, I am able to be still, and know in my whole soul that He is God. This quiet inside myself has allowed Him to teach me. This quiet has allowed me to listen. This quiet has allowed me to trust the flow of life, quit resisting and quit swimming against the current.

In the midst of the most difficult days of 2009, if I tried to explain to someone all the events taking place at the same time, most people would gasp, or cover their mouth in horror, or say something like, "This is just more than anyone should have to go through all at once!"

I will never forget the reaction of one of my dearest friends. After listening to me explain all the events of 2009, she smiled at me and said, "I can't wait to see the work that the Lord is doing inside you!"

Beloved reader, I am sorry for your pain, but I can't wait to see the work that the Lord is doing inside you! Please be still and know that He is God but first, be *still*.

Made in the USA
San Bernardino, CA
01 August 2017